W9-ATA-537

Whales
on the
World Wide Web

Written by Sarah Prince

TM
sundance
A Haights Cross Communications Company

My name is Izzy.
I live in a town
by the sea. Every
spring, whales
swim along the
coastline.

Our class keeps
a record of when
we see whales.
We are learning
as much as we
can about them.
We get lots of
information about
whales from the
World Wide Web.

3

We decided that we would make our own web pages. Then children from other schools can find out about the whales we see.

First we had to decide what information would be interesting to other children.

We made a diagram to show the web pages we would make and how they would be linked.

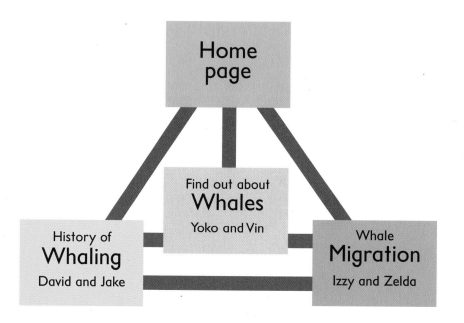

Zelda and I found out about where whales migrate. They travel very long distances each year.

We designed the page on whale migration routes. We included a map that showed where the whales traveled. We linked this map to information about where whales go in the summer and in the winter.

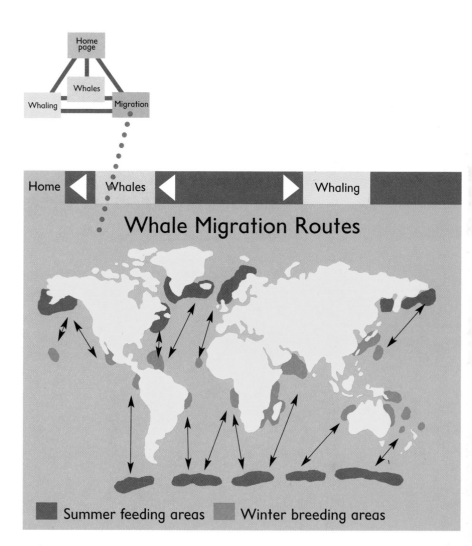

Yoko and Vin found out
what whales look like.

They scanned
photographs of the
whales to use on
their web page.

They labeled the
whales' body parts.

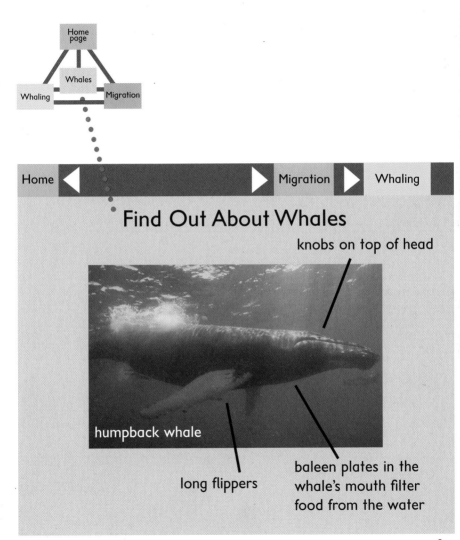

Find Out About Whales

knobs on top of head

humpback whale

long flippers

baleen plates in the whale's mouth filter food from the water

Jake and David found out that in the past many whales were hunted for oil, meat, and whalebone.

While fewer people hunt whales today, whales are still in danger. Some whales get caught in fishing nets and drown. Some whales become sick and die when the places where they live become polluted.

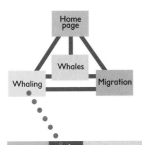

 Home Whales Migration

Whaling

More than 100,000 humpback whales have been killed in the past. Today there are about 12,000 humpback whales. Their population is growing slowly.

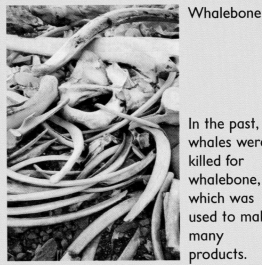

Whalebone

In the past, whales were killed for whalebone, which was used to make many products.

After the pages were designed on the computer, we linked them together.

Our teacher checked what we had done. She said that children from all over the world would visit our site. Then she suggested that we write some information about our class.

13

We added some information about who we were and how to contact us.

We launched our web site on the computer and waited to see if anyone would contact us.

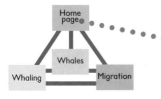

Home   Click to go to: ▶

Humpback Whales at Monterey, California

Welcome to our web site. We are in Grade 2 at the Bayside School. Talk to us about our whales.

Hi,

We really like your web site.

We see humpback whales near our school, too.

We took this picture last year.

How many whales do you see each year?

Mr. Gordon's Class

Williams School

Rock Cove, Maine